AF469081

PASSIONS...

Trekking

PASSIONS...

Trekking

PHOTOGRAPHY BY CLAES GRUNDSTEN

DREAM PLACES YOU'D RATHER BE

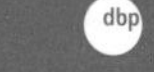

DUNCAN BAIRD PUBLISHERS

LONDON

PASSIONS ... Trekking

First published in the United Kingdom and Ireland in 2007 by
Duncan Baird Publishers Ltd
Sixth Floor
Castle House
75–76 Wells Street
London W1T 3QH

Conceived, created and designed by Duncan Baird Publishers

Managing Editor: Kelly Thompson
Managing Designer: Suzanne Tuhrim
Picture Researcher: Louise Glasson
Editorial Assistant: Kirty Topiwala

British Library Cataloguing-in-Publication Data:
A CIP record for this book is available from the British Library

ISBN: 978-1-84483-385-6

10 9 8 7 6 5 4 3 2 1

Typeset in Bergell and Futura
Colour reproduction by Colourscan, Singapore
Printed in Singapore by Imago

Foreword

THERE IS A CERTAIN SENSE OF FREEDOM THAT COMES FROM SHOULDERING MY RUCKSACK AT THE START OF A DAY. TOGETHER WITH THE ANTICIPATION OF WHERE THAT DAY MAY TAKE ME, THERE IS ALWAYS THE KNOWLEDGE THAT NEW AND MEMORABLE ENCOUNTERS LIE IN THE HOURS AND KILOMETRES AHEAD.

I HAVE ALWAYS LOVED EXPLORING, AND RECALL WITH HUGE FONDNESS MY EARLY "TREKS" AROUND THE FIELDS AND WOODS CLOSE TO MY PARENTS' HOUSE. TO THIS DAY, I REMAIN CAPTIVATED BY THE MOODS AND SEASONS OF THE HILLS NEAR MY HOME, BUT IT IS NOW

MOUNTAINS THE WORLD OVER WHERE I ENGAGE IN MOST OF MY TREKKING ADVENTURES – IN PURSUIT OF ROCKY CLIFFS AND ICY SUMMITS.

WHETHER FACED WITH THE HUMBLING SCALE OF THE GIANT HIMALAYAN PEAKS OR THE VAST EXPANSE OF RACING SKY ABOVE THE PATAGONIAN STEPPE, I AM REMINDED OF THE GREAT FORCES THAT GOVERN OUR EXISTENCE ON THIS PLANET. YET ON ANOTHER LEVEL, THE "SMALLER" THINGS, SUCH AS THE SERENITY OF SUNLIGHT PROBING DEEP INTO A FOREST CANOPY, THE CALMING SOUND OF A RIVER

GENTLY FOLLOWING ITS OWN PATH TOWARD A DISTANT SEA, AN UNEXPECTED GLIMPSE OF A BEAUTIFUL FLOWER OR MAYBE A CHANCE ENCOUNTER WITH THE LOCAL PEOPLE OR WILDLIFE, ALL ADD TO THE RICHNESS OF JOURNEYING THROUGH THESE DIVERSE LANDSCAPES.

TREKKING IS THE PERFECT WAY TO EXPERIENCE FIRST-HAND THE CONSTANT EVOLUTION OF NATURE AND THE PART WE OURSELVES, OR THOSE IN OTHER COUNTRIES OR CULTURES, PLAY IN THE ENVIRONMENT IN WHICH WE LIVE, WORK OR PLAY. WHAT'S MORE, IT CAN BE ENJOYED BY ANYONE WHO IS CAPTIVATED BY THE AMAZING PHOTOGRAPHS IN THIS BOOK: YOUNG

OR OLD, FAST OR SLOW, TIMID OR ADVENTUROUS, LOVERS OF SOLITUDE OR LOVERS OF SHARED EXPERIENCES, AMONG FRIENDS OLD AND NEW ...

IN A HECTIC AGE WHERE THE GAP BETWEEN LEAVING HERE AND GETTING THERE IS OFTEN DEEMED LITTLE MORE THAN AN ENCUMBRANCE, TREKKING OFFERS US ALL THE CHANCE TO ABSORB OURSELVES IN THE JOURNEY ITSELF, CONDUCTED AT OUR OWN PACE SO THAT WE MAY APPRECIATE OUR SURROUNDINGS MORE FULLY. LET YOUR JOURNEY BEGIN ...

DAVE HOLLINGER, *MOUNTAIN INSTRUCTOR AND GUIDE*

"Above all, do not lose your desire to walk. ... I know of no thought so burdensome that one cannot walk away from it."

SØREN KIERKEGAARD (1813–55)

"I often think I know what a walk is going to be like ... but invariably something totally unexpected comes along that takes it far beyond the realms of my imagination."

AGATA BELCEN (1924–)

"The biggest prize in ... hiking is the gift of time. Time to look. Time to think. Time to feel."

CINDY ROSS (1955–)

"Each step is different; only in your mind is it the same."

DAVE HOLLINGER (1974–)

"Walking is man's best medicine."

HIPPOCRATES (C.460–C.370 BC)

"After a day's walk everything has twice its usual value."

GEORGE MACAULAY TREVELYAN (1876–1962)

"I am I plus my surroundings, and if I do not preserve the latter, I do not preserve myself."

JOSE ORTEGA Y GASSET (1883–1955)

"I frequently tramped eight or ten miles through the deepest snow to keep an appointment with a beech tree, or a yellow birch, or an old acquaintance among the pines."

HENRY DAVID THOREAU (1817–62)

"I only went out for a walk and finally concluded to stay out till sundown, for going out, I found, was really going in."

JOHN MUIR (1838–1914)

"Mountains are the beginning and the end of all natural scenery."

JOHN RUSKIN (1819–1900)

"We will stamp on the top with the wind in our teeth ..."

GEORGE MALLORY (1886–1924)

"The only challenge when you walk is yourself."

RUTH HOLLINGER (1977–)

"A huge peak, black
and huge,
As if with voluntary
power instinct,
Upreared its head."

WILLIAM WORDSWORTH (1770–1850)

"... no laboratory, no book, car, train or plane takes the place of honest footwork ..."

DONALD CULROSS PEATTIE (1898–1964)

"The fleeting hour of life of those who love the hills is quickly spent, but the hills are eternal. Always there will be the lonely ridge, the dancing beck, the silent forest ..."

ALFRED WAINWRIGHT (1907–91)

"There is always a beginning and an end but the best part is the journey in between."

ANNIE LEITCH (1928–)

"Any landscape is a condition of the spirit."

HENRI FRÉDÉRIC AMIEL (1812–81)

"If a man does not keep pace with his companions, perhaps it is because he hears a different drummer. Let him step to the music which he hears ..."

HENRY DAVID THOREAU (1817–62)

"When it is darkest, men see the stars."

RALPH WALDO EMERSON (1803–82)

"We have the peculiar privilege ... the freedom to walk this earth, see its beauties, taste its sweetness, partake of its enduring strength."

HAL BORLAND (1900–78)

"Everywhere is walking distance if you have the time."

STEVEN WRIGHT (1955–)

"There's always a period of curious fear between the first sweet-smelling breeze and the time when the rain comes cracking down."

DON DELILLO (1936–)

"Often you set out simply
for a walk yet return with
so much more - a sense of
space, clarity, freedom ..."

NAIMA TAHRI (1875–1930)

"Hiking takes more head than heel."

EMMA GATEWOOD (1887–1973)

"I measure your health by the number of shoes and hats and clothes you have worn out."

RALPH WALDO EMERSON (1803–82)

Locations

All photographs by Claes Grundsten.

page 5 Mont Blanc and Little Lac Chécroui, Italian side
pages 10–11 Alesvagge, Abisko Mountains, Swedish Lapland
page 13 Heaphy River, Heaphy Track, New Zealand
pages 14–15 Rapa Valley, Sarek, Swedish Lapland
pages 16–17 MacDonnell Ranges, Northern Territory, Australia
page 19 Turquoise Coast, Lycian Way, Turkey
pages 20–21 Fish River Canyon, Namibia
page 22 Giant Senecio plant, Mount Kenya, Kenya
page 25 Mount Ama Dablam, Everest Trek
pages 26–27 Kukenan and Roraima, Venezuela
pages 28–29 Between Faralya and Kabak, Lycian Way, Turkey
page 30 Valle Gran Rey, La Gomera, Canary Islands
page 33 Sarvesvagge, Sarek, Swedish Lapland
page 34 Drei Zinnen, Dolomites, Italy
page 37 Forests of Patagonia, Argentina
page 38 Butterfly Valley and Mediterranean Sea, Lycian Way, Turkey

pages 40–41 Temperate Rainforest, Frenchman's Cap, Tasmania
pages 42–43 Monument Valley, Arizona
pages 44–45 Nissunjåkka Creek, Abisko Mountains, Swedish Lapland
page 47 Rautkofel Peak, Dolomites, Italy
pages 48–49 Terikan River, Mulu National Park, Sarawak, Malaysia
pages 50–51 Mer de Glace, Chamonix Valley, France
page 52 Scafell towards Wasdale, Lake District, Great Britain
pages 54–55 Bujuku Valley, Ruwenzori, Uganda
page 57 Gorges Valley from Chogoria Route, Mount Kenya, Kenya
pages 58–59 Rapadalen, Sarek, Swedish Lapland
page 60 Point John, Mount Kenya, Kenya
pages 62–63 American Willowherb, Chilkoot Trail, Canada
pages 64–65 Khuiten Uul, Tavan Bogd National Park, Altai, Mongolia
page 67 Upper Bigo Bogs, Ruwenzori, Uganda
page 68 Khentii Nuruu Mountain Range, Mongolia
pages 70–71 MacKinnons Pass, New Zealand
page 72 Pine Knob, Frenchman's Cap, Tasmania
pages 74–75 Devil's Club, Chilkoot Trail, Alaska

Text credits

Every care has been taken to trace copyright owners, but if we have omitted anyone we apologize and will, if informed, make corrections in any future edition.

page 12 Søren Kierkegaard, from *Kierkegaard's Writing: XXV*. Copyright © Princeton University Press, 1978. Also from Søren Kierkegaard's Journals and Papers, ed. Howard V. Hong and Edna H. Hong. Copyright © Indiana University Press, 1976. **page 23** Cindy Ross, from *Journey on the Crest* (Mountaineers Books, 1987). Copyright © Cindy Ross, 1987. **page 32** George Macaulay Trevelyan, from *The Recreations of an Historian* (T. Nelson and Sons, Ltd., 1919). Copyright © T. Nelson and Sons, Ltd., 1919. **page 35** Jose Ortega y Gasset, from *Meditations on Quixote*, tr. Evelyn Rugg and Diego Marin. Copyright © 1969 and renewed 1989 by W.W. Norton & Company, Inc. **page 66** Donald Culross Peattie, from *The Joy of Walking* (New York Times Magazine, April 1972). Copyright © The New York Times, 1972. **page 69** Alfred Wainwright, from *A Pictorial Guide to the Lakeland Fells, Book Seven: The Western Fells*, (Frances Lincoln Ltd., 1966). Copyright © The Estate of A. Wainwright, 1966. Reproduced by permission of Frances Lincoln Ltd. **page 94** Don DeLillo, from *The Names*, (Picador, 1982). Reprinted by permission of the Wallace Literary Agency, Inc.

About the contributors

DAVE HOLLINGER, FOREWORD

Based in the UK, Dave Hollinger has spent the last 15 years trekking, climbing and mountaineering around the world. He is a member of the Association of Mountaineering Instructors, guiding climbs in the UK as well as leading trips as far afield as the Himalayas, the Karakoram and the Andes. More information can be found at www.ami.org.uk.

CLAES GRUNDSTEN, PHOTOGRAPHER

Claes Grundsten is a trekking specialist and environmental journalist. He has been photographing wilderness areas the world over for more than 30 years, with a particular interest in the mountainous areas of his homeland, Sweden. He is one of Europe's foremost nature photographers and was awarded the World Wildlife's Panda Prize in 2000.